MY SICILIAN NANNA

MY SICILIAN NANNA

A MEMOIR

PETER J. PEDONE SR.

TATE PUBLISHING
AND ENTERPRISES, LLC

My Sicilian Nanna

Published by Tate Publishing & Enterprises, LLC
127 E. Trade Center Terrace | Mustang, Oklahoma 73064 USA
1.888.361.9473 | www.tatepublishing.com

Tate Publishing is committed to excellence in the publishing industry. The company reflects the philosophy established by the founders, based on Psalm 68:11,
"The Lord gave the word and great was the company of those who published it."

Cover design by Joel Uber
Interior design by Jake Muelle

Published in the United States of America

ISBN: 978-1-62746-200-6
Biography & Autobiography / Cultural Heritage
13.06.27

ACKNOWLEDGMENT

This memoir would not have been possible without the encouragement, assistance, and editing by my sister-in-law, Allison Gaye Leak. Allison is a caregiver. She is a registered nurse who retired in the early nineties after serving as senior vice president of patient care services at the Western Pennsylvania Hospital, Pittsburgh, Pennsylvania. She is the matriarch of our family, and we love her!

Thank you, Allison!

TABLE OF CONTENTS

INTRODUCTION

Nanna Portera was my maternal grandmother. Portera is not a common Sicilian surname. Some of Grandma's relatives, including some of her sons and daughters, think it's Spanish. I call this group of relatives the discussion group and will refer to them as the DG (short for discussion group) throughout this book. Some relatives within the DG insisted that the *Cognome* (last name in Italian) Portera is definitely Sicilian, while others do not care either way. Hoping to find an answer, I Googled Portera and found a company that handles antique Spanish doors. Here's what they advertise:

> First we brought you the world's largest collection of antique Spanish doors. Now, we are proud to present our collection of comfortably priced custom doors. Combining old world techniques with modern options, the Portera Custom Door Collection offers entry doors, gates, and interior doors built to your specifications.

The Portera Door Company is located in Pasadena, California, and the closest Nanna Portera or her husband (my grandfather), Franco Portera, or any of his Sicilian family Porteras ever came to Pasadena was San Jose, so I ruled out the possibility of any relationship there. But this could open the door, so to speak, to a possible Spanish connection.

Nanna was born Fara Palazollo around 1883 in a small Sicilian village by the name of Partinico, which at the time was about thirty miles west of Palermo. I also Googled Partinico and discovered it's now (more or less) a suburb of Palermo, destroying my belief that the United States held the patent for sprawl growth. Nanna didn't know the exact date of her birth. When asked, she responded that her birth date was not important. Her birth date only mattered to God and her paternal family, and since she was no longer with her paternal family, it mattered to no one. The DG suggested that Nanna was perhaps concealing her age for one of two reasons: one, because she wanted to appear younger, or two, maybe she was older than her husband and didn't want anyone to know that. Who knows? I guess someday we could find out the date of her birth and baptism by visiting Partinico and checking with the local Catholic churches or we could join Ancestry.com and start the search there, but that's something none of us have ventured to do or even planned for. I guess in a way, that's like admitting Nanna's opinion was the final word on the subject.

Nanna and her husband Franco (Frank) immigrated to the United States in 1913. My Grandfather Frank is the guy with the original last name of Portera, so the same group of relatives mentioned above, the DG, holds him responsible for the family controversy (discussions) over the nationality of the name. Nanna turned a deaf ear to the rumblings of the DG. I guess she felt her involvement was rather minor, and she was simply involved by marital association; therefore, she had nothing to do with it.

This photo of Nanna and Grandpa Franco was taken in Buffalo, NY around 1916, the year my mother Mary was born. Now that I look at this photo more closely, I can see a wee bit of Spanish in Franco (just kidding).

We grandkids called Grandma Nanna. Later we discovered nanna is an Americanization of *nonna*, the correct Italian word for grandma. Anyway, Nanna married young (the DG estimates between the ages of fourteen to sixteen) as was the custom in Sicily at the time and was already the mother of three children when she immigrated to the United States. The number of children would grow to seven quickly as a result of using the rhythm method of birth control. One of these children was my mother. Because Nanna and Frank were poor, her immigration to the United States was accomplished in stages. Frank sailed directly from Palermo to New York to get a job and earn money, while Grandma waited in Tunis, Tunisia, Africa, until funds were sufficient to bring her and the three kids to the United States. Why Tunis, you ask? I'll get to that later.

While I'm at it, let me say that I plan to present Nanna's experiences in life along with her advice and remedies for a better life in an integrated fashion. I will talk about her life experiences and then integrate the advice and remedies she practiced and preached. Imagine the changes this woman experienced: she migrated from Sicily to the United States with three children at her side; she lived in a bleak, cold environment among strangers for three years in Buffalo, New York. She traveled by train in third class with four children from the east coast of the United States to the west coast, and all this time, she was not able to speak one word of English. She experienced more in her first four years in the United States than some other ten people might experience in a lifetime. I feel this is important to recognize so that the reader will better understand that although Nanna's life had so many significant changes, the strength of her values, morals, and, more importantly, her beliefs (imparted to her by her illiterate parents and the ingrained society of rural Catholic Sicily) changed not one iota. Whatever her parents taught her in the late nineteenth century was still as valid to her in 1965, the year she died, as it was in 1883 or whatever year she was born. Nanna never changed, and although we children believed her every word at first, we learned better as we grew older.

Perhaps holding tightly to those very values, morals, and beliefs is what enabled Nanna to survive those terribly lonely and frightening times! Her kitchen, her garden, and her Italian community were her sanctuaries. Like the Mexican Barrios of today, her community of like-minded friends provided her with the security and sense of being home. She had no need to venture forth, learn English, and pursue the lifestyle of her new American surroundings. Living in little Italy provided her the security and confidence she needed to be herself and to take the time to pass onto her grandchildren the beliefs she thought essential to their very survival in this world and the next.

Grandma's birth name was Fara (which means beautiful in Arabic), which further stoked the buzz about nationality between members of the DG. The DG now advanced the theory that Nanna was part Arab, and Frank was Spanish, so therefore there was very little Sicilian between them. The Arab theory held forth for many years. However shortly after the tragic events of the 9/11 Arab terrorist attacks on New York, that subject and theory was moved to the back burner. If still talked about today, it's in a very hushed manner. A saving grace in the family discussion over ethnicity is that Nanna's maiden name was Palazollo, which is Sicilian without question, but "behind the doors" questions about the Spanish and Arab connections remained until her death.

When speaking of Sicily, it would be easier to list the empires and countries that never occupied her than listing those that have. Sicily is the largest island in the Mediterranean. Conquering and occupying her became a trophy quest for any sea-faring nation desiring to add a bit of real estate to their inventory. We could start of course with the Vikings who were renowned for their lighting quick raids and their raping, pillaging, and plundering throughout the Mediterranean area. Thanks to those Vikings, there are many Sicilians today with blue eyes and red and blonde hair. Although brutal in their social manners, the Vikings did manage to infuse a bit of lighter-colored skin to the early occupants of Sicily who probably had the same physical appearance as most of the folks we would find there today (sans the blue eyes and lighter hair).

Early history tells us Sicily's first occupiers were the Greeks, who made the island a colony, and it remained as such until around 750 BC when the Romans took it away from them. It remained a place to be conquered until it was officially united with Italy in 1860. Keep in mind that not too far south of Sicily is Arabia, and the Arabs, like many others, had their turn to occupy Sicily probably around the same time they occupied Spain. And let us not forget Napoleon and the French island of Corsica, a bit north of Sicily—they had their turn as well. So taking all these various facts into consideration makes it more understandable why the DG had their doubts about ethnicity in Sicily. Add all these cultures together with their various recipes and cooking styles, and you can probably rest assured that Sicily has some of the best restaurants in the world!

Fara had no formal education—none whatsoever. Her training and education took place in the family kitchen. Grandma was like most young Sicilian girls growing up in Sicily at the time who were trained to be *casalingas* (housewives). Only the daughters of the very wealthy received a formal education. When Nanna arrived in the United States, she could not speak or write a word of English. This didn't seem to bother her. As long as she had access to the kitchen, she was fine.

Everything I say about Nanna is true—well perhaps some of the family folklore may twist things a bit, but it is not too farfetched. Grandma was so much fun and full of love to be around, but she could also be a bitch, something like a cross between Jean Stapleton and Kathy Bates. For example, after her daughters married and when opportunity presented itself, she would visit their homes and inspect for cleanliness. Her favorite drills were to inspect for food crumbs under tablecloths or to check for dust on windowsills. Quite often, she could be found in cupboards and pantries inspecting pots and pans for food film around the edges. If any transgressions were discovered, she would admonish the guilty daughter in front of every person in the house, especially the daughter's husband. Husbands of daughters were infallible and claimed a status almost equal to that of a Sicilian son. However, when it came to the daughters, she gloated with pleasure whenever she was able to reduce them to tears. That was the bitchy Kathy Bates part of her.

Nanna also spied on us grandkids. When not inspecting pantries, she could be found, on occasion, sneaking up on us kids to ensure we were not playing house. In later years when she came to live with my mom and dad, she would quietly stalk up the stairs to peek into my room or my sister's room to ensure we were not playing with ourselves or doing some other dirty deed. At times, Grandma could be a saintly woman (especially in front of guests), and at other times, she could be the perfect bitch as stated earlier. Whatever character she chose to be, I loved her very much.

Although she was a giant of a woman in the eyes of her grandchildren, Nanna was a diminutive four feet, eleven inches tall—stretched out on a stretching rack. In later years, she tried very hard to round herself out to 4 × 4, but she did not live long enough to achieve that goal. Her blue eyes combined with her black hair gave her a very bewitching look that had the capability of freezing us grand kids in place, and we dared not run away from her because her little legs moved faster than Superman's speeding bullet. And when she caught us, she was not afraid to lay a couple of whacks on the butt—in fact that was an ass-sure-ity! That's Nanna in the photo below with five of her seven children. Steve is in the back row to the left of Nanna; Paul is on her right. In the front row, left to right, are Josephine, John, and Katherine. You can see that the kids were already beginning to leave her in the dust when it comes to height, but that was the only place.

Many novels have been written about immigrants and their experiences in coming to America. Essentially, you can find an immigration story for every nationality found in America today. Examples would be: *The Godfather* and *The Mafia* for Italians, *The Good Earth* for Scandinavians, *Journey of Hope* for the Irish, and *The Turtle Catcher* for the Germans. I have read many of these novels and enjoyed them immensely, but all too often, I found more than a bit of sadness in each. In many of these novels, the storyline followed a familiar pattern: the mother or father of the first generation works his/her fingers to the bone to get their kids an education, only to find, despite all family efforts, many of the kids turn to crime or some other form of self-destruction. Then there is just the opposite: one or two of the kids goes to college and become famous. Same old stuff. What's missing in these stories is the ethnic humor that came across the sea in the same boat with each of the various nationalities that journeyed to America. Kissing the Blarney Stone for the Irish- and Italian-themed movies starring Joe Pesci are good examples of the humor I'm thinking about.

There were hardships for sure, but all these immigrants had a drive and a reason for facing the hardships associated with each voyage. That drive was the freedom that awaited them on American soil. Although my maternal grandparents had many a hardship in establishing their lives in the United States, there was always room for humor, and hopefully, I can bring some of that humor forward in this book. I hope I succeed, and I hope you enjoy it.

PS: Unless I make an obvious distinction, I will sometimes refer to Nanna as grandma and/or grandmother. She preferred to be called Nanna, but as we grandkids immersed ourselves in American culture and our knowledge of the English language improved, we began to call her grandma or grandmother. I should make myself clearer here: for many of us grandkids, to include myself, our first language was Sicilian/Italian—I still get confused at times. However, whatever we called Nanna, she understood all the various titles.

CHAPTER 1

THE FIRST STAGE OF IMMIGRATION PARTINICO TO TUNIS

Men can be clever at times. Women are always clever.

—Nanna Portera

Frank departed for New York from Palermo in 1913. After clearing Ellis Island, he made his way to the home of friends in Buffalo, New York. This was customary for most Italian immigrants—they knew someone or the friend of someone who would house them until they were financially secure enough to find their own residence, and then the procedure would start all over again, and the previously hosted would take on the role of host to yet another immigrant. This pattern of immigration accounted for many of the laborers who would form the workforce for emerging US factories and also would provide the forefathers of most Italian restaurant chefs and owners.

Pizza came later. This same procedure was used by other immigrating groups such as the Irish and Germans. We all know the stories—we've read all the books and seen all the movies. Please, no more Mafia movies!

Okay, so Frank jumped on a passenger liner and made his way to Buffalo via Ellis Island. Meanwhile, back in Tunis, Nanna is nurturing and guarding her three children: Katherine, the oldest; Josephine, the second; and Paul, the third. Now apparently, so the story goes, Frank is dillydallying about Buffalo while Nanna guards the virginity of her two daughters and son in Tunis. Why Tunis, you ask? Because one of Frank's cousins was a wealthy merchant there, and he agreed to house Nanna and the children until Frank sent the funds to transport them to the United States. The family has since lost personal contact with this cousin, but the fact that he existed stoked even more the discussions about a trace of Arab blood in the family. As mentioned earlier, discussions of this nature fell off considerably after 9/11.

But wait, Frank is taking too much time to accumulate the necessary funds to bring his family over. He seems to be enjoying himself free of Nanna's watchful eyes and free of the responsibility of watching over his two daughters. The son is no problem, it's the daughters.

Nanna's no dummy. She knows Italian men, and she knows one named Franco extremely well, so she uses applied psychology. She knows her husband, so she applies what works. She sends Franco the following letter—who wrote it for her, I know not.

> Caro Marito (dear husband):
>
> The Weather here in Tunis has been beautiful, and the girls, Paul and I have gone for several walks to the market place and back, and sometimes we stroll around the central park. I have noticed of late how the men have been attracted to Katherine. I first noticed this when several men in Turbans began following us and waving at us every time we looked back at them. Oh well, she's now in her teens, so I guess we must learn to accept this fact that men are going to be interested in her.
>
> We miss you very much and hope you will soon have the funds to pay for our trip to America. We can hardly wait to hear from you and our urge to come to America is very strong.
>
> Love,
> Your faithful wife Fara.

It's assumed that Nanna and the kids spent about six months in Tunis. In any event, it was enough time to wear on the nerves of all concerned—cousins or not. Well about a month or so after Nanna sent this letter, funds in the amount of $500 arrived; her letter did the trick, and much to the relief of the hosting cousin, Nanna and the children were on their way to America.

You may be wondering at this point how did Nanna and her children get to Tunis? By Tramp Steamer, that's how. Franco took a regular passenger liner, and Nanna took a tramp steamer. The sailors on the tramp steamer took a liking to Nanna and the girls, so one of them gave up his cabin to her; it was a brief trip, but nevertheless, Nanna had a way about her. They managed to eat well also. The trip from Palermo to Tunis was such a good experience that Nanna and Frank's wealthy cousin decided that Nanna and the kids should travel to the United States by the same means. Passage on tramp steamers cost less and was considered more reliable and safe than passenger liners. Perhaps this line of thinking was supported by the fact that a passenger liner with the name *Titanic* was lost at sea just one year before Nanna and the kids left Partinico.

CHAPTER 2

EARLY ESTABLISHED BELIEFS OR THE INFLUENCE PARENTS HAVE FOREVER

NANNA PORTERA'S ADVICE AND HEALTH REMEDIES: SEXUAL ACTIVITY

Never underestimate the difficulty of changing false beliefs by facts.

—Economist Henry Rosovsky

As soon as we were old enough to understand, Nanna's first bit of advice for perfect health was that virginity until marriage for women was a godly requirement. Women who lost their virginity prior to marriage would live a life of prostitution. No Sicilian male of any worth would want to marry a woman who has been with another man. Sexual activity prior to marriage for men was not only okay but would enhance future sexual performance when married. Remedy: women *no*, men *yes*.

DISCUSSION

Sicilian men were created in God's image. Their charm and good looks makes them irresistible. Therefore it's understandable how difficult it would be for women, especially white, Anglo-Saxon Protestant women, to resist their advances. Keeping score of conquests and talking about it later was perfectly acceptable. Women should not find sexual activity enjoyable. Sexual activity exists only to create more Sicilian males. An occasional weak conception may result in the birth of a Sicilian female, but that's God's will.

MORE DISCUSSION

At first, a weak conception may be thought of as a low sperm count, but this is contrary to the virility normally associated with Sicilian men. It is more reasonable to assume therefore that weak conception was more than likely caused by some fertility problem in the female. Perhaps too much female enjoyment was demonstrated during the act that somehow obstructed the flow of sperm, or something to that effect, is a better explanation.

Nudity around the house was okay and actually encouraged for men but a definite no-no for women. Men parading about the house naked, especially well-endowed men, was perfectly acceptable and actually a joy for proud mothers and grandmothers to see. A Sicilian expression existed to discourage women from prancing about the house naked or even partially dressed, "Mettiti un bel vestito e fatti bella; anche l'occhio vuole la sua parte. Non basta essere intelligenti."

"Put on a nice dress and pretty yourself up. Appearances count. It's not enough to be intelligent." Enough said.

DISCUSSION

My male cousins and I felt that Grandma's sexual remedy (read advice) was excellent. We practiced it as often as possible. On the other hand, Grandma's advice for my female cousins must have been difficult for them to accept. Being as beautiful as they were, I'm sure they found themselves in situations where the urge to have sex was often suppressed by the fear that having sex would surely lead to a life of prostitution. Surely if they gave in and had sex, word would soon be out that they were easy scores, so the dilemma must have been difficult for them to live with. I can't imagine any of them, being as hot-blooded as I think they were, could remain virgins until the time of their weddings. Nevertheless, apparently they made the grade because they managed to be married in white gowns (implied purity), and that meant a great deal to them as well as Nanna.

For some of us, facts never dispelled the false beliefs.

Referring back to this chapter will be made frequently.

CHAPTER 3

THE SECOND STAGE OF IMMIGRATION TUNIS TO BUFFALO, NEW YORK

WELCOME TO AMERICA

Nanna and her kids arrived at Ellis Island well nourished. She managed to make friends with all the Italian seamen on the tramp steamer and was able to gather extra food from them for herself and the kids. She and the kids arrived in America without passports; therefore, they were quickly given the title of WOPs (without passports). The fact that they arrived without passports, which was theoretically illegal, didn't seem to matter to the immigration authorities. Apparently, the need for common laborers in emerging American factories meant more to the government of the United States than did existing immigration laws. In any event, upon their arrival, they posed for photos, were examined for signs of the flu and/or other respiratory diseases, and released almost immediately to Franco, who had arrived earlier with salami sandwiches and plenty of French bread.

They made their way to the train station where they embarked for Franco's pad in Buffalo. They would remain in Buffalo close to three years saving their money for a start-up life and train fare to San Jose, California, where Franco could get a job pruning fruit trees in the orchards of the Santa Clara Valley. Word was sent ahead to other Italian families in San Jose that the Porteras were on their way there, so various Italian families began to prepare for their arrival. My mother, Mary (same as Paul McCartney's), was born while they lived in Buffalo. She was brought into this world by Maria Forestino, a midwife of good repute, who served the needs of all the Sicilians and other Italians who lived in little Italy on the slummy fringes of Buffalo. It seemed as though every immigrant in Buffalo was working and saving money so they could depart that cold and windy city as soon as possible. Nothing much has changed in Buffalo.

It's 1917 now, and WWI occupies the thoughts of people worldwide. Franco and Fara are thankful that Paul is still too young to be drafted and the girls, to include my mother, Mary, are all healthy. Now they have the funds and connections to book train fare to paradise—*California here we come!* Reports of how beautiful and similar to Sicily California is has excited them beyond description.

Italians, especially Sicilians, do not do well in a cold and snowy climate. They couldn't wait to get to the land of milk and honey. Buffalo would be a good future home for the football team, to be called The Buffalo Bills, but nothing else, especially not Sicilians.

CHAPTER 4

EARLY ESTABLISHED BELIEFS (ADVICE) ABOUT THE WORLD ACCORDING TO NANNA

The most remarkable of truths about Italians: no truth existed beyond personal experience, and all evidence that contradicted personal belief was to be dismissed.

—Donna Leon, *Dressed for Death*, p. 110

Most every time my cousins and I would be at Nanna's house, she would give us lessons on how the world operated. She gained our attention by feeding us while giving us our lessons. Her favorite treat, which became our favorite treat, was her homemade Italian bread freshly baked and heavily coated with olive oil, with just a little sprinkling of salt on the oil. There was no limit on how much we could eat. Whatever our *stomachis* (stomachs) could hold was ours for the having. I think it was here, in Nanna's kitchen, that I learned that food was good, especially Italian food cooked like Nanna cooked it. To say I like food is grossly understated—I love food. Food is part of my DNA. Today, thanks to Nanna's cooking, my wife and I will drive hundreds of miles to eat at a restaurant endorsed by the likes of Emeril Lagasse or Bobby Flay. We are true foodies! Grazie, Nanna!

Back to Nanna's kitchen. First, my cousins and I learned that all wars—every war that ever hit the planet Earth—was caused by the *Tedescis* (the Germans). She demonstrated to us how the German troops would march in a goose-step fashion, and she held her right hand with extended index finger over her head to indicate the spike on the helmets of the German soldiers. That lesson was repeated every time we gathered in her kitchen. My female cousins were warned never to date or even think about marrying a German man for surely he will be in some future war that he himself probably started. Nanna would stare at the girls and, with what seemed to be terror in her eyes, would say in a low, trembling voice: "Sta in guardia! I Tedesci sonno acqua chete, e potrebbe fari del male!" (Watch it! The Germans are sly and could be harmful to you.)

The second major lesson was that all Orientals ate cats and dogs. We were admonished never to eat in a Chinese or Japanese restaurant because the chicken listed on the menu was more than likely the dogs and cats that have recently been reported as missing in the neighborhood.

The mysterious disappearance of these household pets was directly attributable to the Chinese family living down the street from her. These very same Oriental people carried large cleavers around under their aprons and would occasionally capture wayward children and butcher them as well as the local missing population of cats and dogs. "So who knows," she said, "if you eat at one of these restaurants, you may be eating your best friend who has recently been reported as missing or your neighbor's cat." Lesson learned: stay away from Oriental people and never, ever eat at a Chinese or Japanese restaurant. My mother, who was schooled in these very same worldly facts long before my cousins and I, took Nanna's advice seriously, and she never ate at any Oriental restaurant. She died in 2006 at age ninety-two, and seriously, she never ate at an Oriental restaurant. If you don't believe me, ask my wife; she'll vouch for that!

A third lesson was that Turkos, like the one pictured on the Sanka coffee can, abducted and brutalized small children. Should we ever see a man walking around with a Turban on his head, we would then quickly run the other way or, better yet, find our mother and father as quickly as we can and let them know that a Turko is in the area. Turkos do not believe in God or Jesus. Their God is another Turko who also wears a turban, and when they die, you can be certain they will go to hell.

I am reminded of this every time I see a Sanka coffee can in an antique Store.

Over the years, the discussion group (DG) discussed Nanna's lesson about the Arab on the coffee can. Her hateful attitude toward the Turko, they reasoned, seemed to dispel the rumor that Nanna was part Arab. The DG seemed to be split right down the middle on this subject—one half supported the "no Arab" theory, while the other half thought it was a ploy used by her to give that impression. The DG knew Nanna very well!

The fourth lesson was that blacks were best at entertaining people—they were not much good for anything else. They were essentially *buffanos* (clowns). Some of them were really Germans in disguise.

Those who were pure black could be seen often eating watermelons and fried chicken. If you were confused, it would be because Germans were very crafty people, and they could pass as black entertainers by painting their faces with black shoe polish, thus appearing to be blacks and as such could win over the minds of those they were entertaining.

DISCUSSION

As I think back on this, I guess Nanna was thinking propaganda, and thinking that if the Germans could fool you and win over your mind, it would be easier for them to convince you that war was necessary. Nanna's hatred of Germans was really, really deep-seated—understandably, it never changed. As most people realize, Italy, to include Sicily, fought on the Allied side in the war against Germany. If Nanna was indeed born in 1883, she would have been thirty-five when WWI ended in 1918, by which time Italy had suffered 600,000 death, 950,000 wounded, and 250,000 wounded for life. Perhaps she even knew some of those casualties from her own family and village of Partinico. No wonder she hated the Germans!

Nanna had nicknames for all us male grandkids. The girls were not as lucky: Marie was Marie, Fay was Fay, and Kathy was Caterina (Italian for Katherine). Nanna didn't like it that her girl grandchildren should have Americanized names. If you were given an Italian name as Italians should be, then that's what you should be called. This was another of Nanna's no-nonsense approaches. My cousin Frank, the oldest Portera male cousin, was called Frankgootso (I'll try to spell them out phonetically). She had no nickname for George, and his feelings were really hurt. Cousin Nat was Natalaydo, Joe was Peppeedo, and I was Peedough. These various names were totally acceptable to us, and surely it should make sense to anyone who heard them. Peedough is as good as Peter any day!

This is a photo of me and my cousins—that's Nanna's house in the background. Looking left to right starting in the back row, that's Joe (Peppeedo); then George (no nick name), George's Brother Frank, called Frankgootso, and Nat (Natalaydo). Front row: that's me, first one in the front row. I'm the small guy; next is Kathy (Caterina), then Fay, and finally Marie. Joe and George (first and second in the back row), and Nat (last in the back row) and Kathy, next to me in the first row are no longer on this planet.

Other lessons were provided throughout the years, but they always concluded with what we cousins referred to as the final lesson, and that was that virginity in women was perhaps the most important thing we should be aware of. We males were to ensure that our wives would be healthy, pious Sicilian virgins. Women and men of other nationalities could only be dated but never ever taken seriously. When we male cousins were alone with Nanna, it was made perfectly clear that if we were going to screw anyone, make sure it was a white, Anglo-Saxon protestant and not a good, clean Italian or Sicilian girl. Please refer to chapter 1 for more details on this subject. More of Nanna's advice and remedies will appear in subsequent chapters.

CHAPTER 5

EARLY ESTABLISHED BELIEFS (ADVICE) THE ROLE OF WOMEN

There is only one place for women, and it's called the kitchen.

—Nanna Portera

Nanna believed that women were born to raise children and provide for their families. Education for women was in the kitchen. Should you insist that this chapter be removed, you are essentially ignoring my point. Nanna believed all women belonged in the kitchen, no exceptions.

CHAPTER 6

THE THIRD STAGE OF IMMIGRATION BUFFALO, NEW YORK, TO SAN JOSE, CALIFORNIA

It is said in family folklore that Paul was a spoiled brat. He was the number one son and obviously the person to inherit whatever the family had when Nanna and Frank went to Catholic heaven. Paul was prepared to take on that role even at age nine. One time, when asked where he was going as the third class train coach rambled through mid-America, Paul responded: "To take a shit." Paul and his siblings were learning English much faster than his parents. Actually, he was on his way to solicit money from passengers who felt sorry for the Italian family traveling with so many unruly kids. He probably played the role to perfection, staring at people who were eating their lunches so that they would offer him a sandwich or two. He remained talented in that way until his death in 1977 at age sixty-three. He died of cancer caused by heavy smoking. Paul's parents died long before he did, but there was no inheritance to be had. The money was used up in supporting and raising his younger siblings long before he bit the dust. He would not have inherited much anyway.

Members of the Italian club were present at the San Jose railroad depot when the Porteras arrived at their destination. Kisses were exchanged, the family was packed up into various modes of transportation, and then they were shuffled off to the home of Pietro and Salvatrice Pedone, who later would become my other set of grandparents—families were tight then. My dad, Mario John Pedone, was only two years old when the Porteras arrived, so I was just a gleam in his eye at the time, but some of that gleam was also for my mother, Mary, who was still a baby in Nanna's arms.

The Pedone home was located on Illinois Avenue in San Jose. Today, it continues to shelter new immigrants to this country. It is the home of Mexican immigrants who work at cleaning floors in plants where computers are made. There are no more fruit orchards in San Jose or in Santa Clara County. The Valley as it was called back then was nothing but prunes and apricots when the Porteras arrived. Today, the Valley is no longer called the Santa Clara Valley. No, after man cut all the fruit trees down and built huge industrial plants that generated massive quantities of industrial waste, it is now appropriately called

Silicone Valley. What used to be one of the most pristine locations on earth is now nothing more than a polluted mess of freeways, shopping malls, and fast-food joints. But I digress.

Grandpa Frank immediately went to work making good money as a pruning specialist, or arborist if you like. He was very talented at orchard work as were most Sicilians at the time. They had a natural instinct for what branches to trim and what suckers to cut off for the tree to produce as much fruit as possible. Frank would be shuttled from one orchard to the next by my other and future grandfather, Pietro Pedone. Pietro was a hustler and a mobster but very kind to his fellow Sicilians.

After Pietro's arrival in San Jose in 1913, he had soon discovered that ranchers were in critical need of arborists, so he organized an all-Sicilian arborist crew and employed them through the contracts he made with local ranchers—a good deal for him as well as the Sicilians he employed. On the side, Grandpa Pedone also made some wine that in the future would generate even greater revenues when prohibition hit the streets—that is, he made good money until several bullets to the head ended his life at a Shell gas station on San Carlos Street, but more on that and life in America and San Jose later.

CHAPTER 7

PHYSICAL REMEDIES—PRICKLY PEARS

Prickly pears (*Opuntia ficus-indica*) grow as abundantly in Sicily as they do in India. "Ficus-Indica" translates in Italian as fig of India. If you have never eaten a fig of India, you don't know what you are missing. For sake of brevity, please permit me to refer to this delectable cactus fruit as cacti—thank you. Sicilians love cacti. To watch a Sicilian despine cacti is like watching Michelangelo paint. The cacti is cut off its paddle-shaped branch with a twist of the hand, and while the hand is protected from the spines by newspaper, the skin of the cacti is split down the middle and peeled off, revealing the fruit within. Nanna was a master at removing the spines of cacti. When Nanna went to harvest cacti, we kids knew a treat was coming. We would follow close behind her as she cleaned and handed each of us a tasty morsel. The cacti fruit comes in various colors, primarily red, yellow, and green. The color of our lips revealed the color of the last one consumed.

Nanna's veggie of choice, the fig of India plant, commonly referred to as the prickly pear plant, is pictured here. Look at the photo closely; see the long, sharp paddle thorns? Falling into a grouping of this ficus-India plant was very painful indeed, but the medicinal benefits were unbelievable, and they tasted great. Nanna and her miracle cures came on the scene long before Doctor Oz. She could have been a contender and quite the attraction on national television.

To say Nanna grew cacti would be a gross understatement. She not only grew cacti, she nurtured each plant to perfection. The plants doubled as a fence surrounding her and Frank's property—a real discouragement to potential intruders. Her yard looked like the Mojave Desert with cacti growing as far as the eye could see. Cacti did not serve as food and security only—do not be mistaken. Cacti also had its medicinal purposes. Sicilians tended to immigrate to climates where prickly pears (another name for cacti) were sure to grow, and California was such a place.

Along with being taught everyday household tasks by her mother, Nanna had also received training in every conceivable health remedy. Household illnesses or accidents were a matter of life or death for poor people around the world—Portinico not excluded. Outdoor plants and herbs were the local pharmacy. Ancient formulas were used to concoct salves and drinks that served as cure-alls for common ailments. Medical remedies grew in the countryside. Doctors were virtually unknown in Portinico, so families compensated for this lack of medical attention by specializing in the treatment of certain ailments. The Rizzos, for example, specialized in ear infections and the Tomasellos in body bruises and broken bones. Nanna's family, the Palazollos, specialized in salves that reduced swellings, bruises, and infectionsm, in other words, skin ailments.

One family favorite was the salves and concoctions derived from *nopal* (no-pahl), the aforementioned paddle-shaped branch upon which the cacti fruit grew. Nopal is also good to eat, tasting like green beans and bell peppers with the texture of okra. Paddles that are at least eight inches in length taste the best. To cook or use to make salves, remove the paddles' thorns with a vegetable peeler (wearing protective gloves), then slice and sauté with onions, melt in some cheese of your choice, and eat with tortillas or nice, thick French bread.

Instead of eating all the nopal she cooked, Nanna would whip up a large amount of her harvest (as in whipped potatoes) and then added various herbs to it to use as a salve to suck up boils or other skin ailments that occasionally infected family and neighbors. She would whip up these concoctions over a high heat on the wood stove, then wrap them securely around the affected area, and voila, a cure would occur in a day or two. The infection seemed to disappear overnight. When removed, the bandage would contain all the goo and infected material that caused the problem in the first place. We kids used to watch Nanna treat her patients and utter oohs and aahs as she removed the bandage—we couldn't wait to see the puss and gore within the wrapping, and then the girls would scream, and the guys would say, "Hey, nice job, Nanna, you got all that shit out!"

"Non si parle cosi," she would admonish. (Don't speak like that.)

CHAPTER 8

LIFE IN SAN JOSE—PART 1

Between the years 1916 to 1922, Nanna and Frank had three more children—all boys, making a total of seven kids in the family. Their names in order of birth were: Steve, John, and Sam. This total was good for the church and ultimately good for America because it added three more young men to the thousands of young men that would be drafted to fight World War II. Their births also added to the number of future breadwinners now within the Portera family. With nine mouths to feed, the young men typically had to get out and start working early. Some did and some didn't, but the prevailing thought back then was that having four boys to help support the family was a very good thing. The three girls on the other hand were considered quite a burden.

I might add that any mother having four children after the age of thirty is considered to be at higher risk for birth complications, so having four kids at that age, while having to care for a growing number of other children, must have been exhausting! I guess this speaks volumes for Nanna's strength of character.

The Porteras purchased a home and acreage on San Carlos Street, almost directly across the street from the O'Connors Hospital, where my grandfather Frank moonlighted as a gardener and grounds keeper. Here again his gardening and arborist skills paid off handsomely, and the extra money helped negate the need to take the boys out of school to help support the family. Instead, the extra money helped to keep them in school until their graduation from high school, which was not common for Sicilian families at the time. Son John proved to be the best student, and after graduation from Stanford (yes, Stanford), he became a high school teacher in Huston, California—a one-horse town at the time. It was quite an achievement for a family that really didn't believe in education! Later, John would be drafted and commissioned a lieutenant in the army and would serve in the European theatre of operations, as did his Brother Sam. Both made it home safely. Paul and Steve never served in the military because of some health reasons. I believe both were determined by army medical authorities to be 4F (unsuited for military service) because of stomach ulcers. Sicilian men tend to get ulcers easily because they worry too much about their images.

I have many pleasant memories of Grandpa's working at the hospital. When I was five years old, my dad was out of work and my parents could not afford a rental, so we lived with my grandparents on San Carlos Street. This pleased me enormously because I would get more freshly buttered bread than my cousins would since I was right there living with the source. I was sure my cousins were jealous, and this was yet another reason to be happy—that was one good memory. Other great memories included playing in Grandpa Franco's garden. I'm sure he didn't like that, but for me, it meant an endless supply of fresh tomatoes and strawberries and anything else that appealed to me at the time, including green almonds and ripe walnuts. It was a veritable feast. When Franco came home from work and found me prowling in his garden, he would get very angry and chase me in order to apply a few whacks to the butt. However, I was much faster than he, and I could climb the various fruit trees much quicker than he could retrieve a long stick to whack me with. I found that it usually took about ten minutes for his anger to subside, and then it would be safe for me to climb down. Later, I would sit in his lap, and he would feed me more buttered bread.

The Porteras and the Pedones became inseparable. Sundays would find them assembled in some park or in someone's orchard barbequing sausages and boiling water for pasta. Occasionally T-bone steaks were on the menu, especially if there was something to celebrate, such as a pending wedding of one of the girls. The first

Portera daughter to go was Josephine. She married an Italian fisherman by the name of Sam Russo from North Beach in San Francisco, and they later produced two of my favorite cousins, Natalie (called Natalaydo) and Marie. The Russos called it quits after having only two kids, which was very unusual for Sicilians at the time. Perhaps the realization that it was expensive to raise kids in the United States was finally sinking in despite what the church said.

The second Portera daughter to marry was Katherine, who married a Sicilian handyman by the name of Dominic Rizzo. They also had two kids: cousins Joe (called Peppeedo) and Kathy (short for Katherine or Caterina). The Rizzos settled in San Jose, and that's where they remained until the entire family passed away, one by one from cancer. My cousin Kathy suffered a great deal with a very vicious form of pancreatic cancer. Kathy and I were born four days apart. She was born on December 4, 1934, and I was born on December 8. We were very close and often double-dated during our high school days. I visited with her during her final days in a cancer treatment facility and was able to say good-bye to this much-loved cousin of mine. After Kathy's death, which was preceded by the deaths of her parents and Brother Joe, and counting the death of my uncle Paul, the score was cancer 5, my Sicilian relatives 0.

As you can see, my Cousin Kathy was quite beautiful. She suffered greatly, and died much too young—I miss you Kathy!

My uncle Paul, the one who said shit on the train to San Jose from Buffalo, led a typical first generation Sicilian life in San Jose. He met Frances Tragni at some Italian/American festivity in downtown San Jose, and they married shortly thereafter—I think that was about 1924. Paul found a niche in the local economy by providing a service transporting old tires to tire recapping facilities located in southern California. He prospered, driving old tires down south, getting them recapped, and then reselling them in northern California. Paul was ingenious that way and never changed. My dad used to say that Paul could squeeze a nickel and get a quarter. He and Frances provided me with yet another two cousins, Frank (called Frankgootso) and George (who remained pissed off all his life because he had no nickname). Frank was the only one named after my grandfather Franco because there were still some sensitive feelings about ethnic origin, and Franco was still thought by some members of the family to be Spanish—he was a nice man and everyone loved him, but there was still that lingering doubt about his Sicilian purity.

Here's a photo of my Cousin George on a Pony. We all loved to play Cowboys and Indians. George remained pissed-off all his life because Nanna did not give him a nick-name.

Let me pause here a minute to mention the two children factor. Early on, I gained the impression that second generation Sicilians quickly learned that having kids could be expensive and that large numbers of children only benefited the church, not the family. Keep in mind that most of this history took place during the great depression, so jobs and money were tight. Families began to realize that having kids was expensive, and even though it was against religious teachings, the Portera children (my aunts and uncles) learned quickly that safe sex also meant fewer kids, so one form or another of birth control was used by all of them, including my parents.

Nanna, in the meantime, was in her glory. The prickly pear fence was growing by leaps and bounds, and the Cacti fruit was in abundance. She even convinced Franco to plant a mulberry tree that produced the juiciest mulberries I have ever tasted. But wait; I digress again. Nanna's yard, which was about six or seven acres, soon transformed in appearance from bare acreage in San Jose to a Sicilian ranch in Portinico. Have you ever heard of capers? Nanna grew capers as well as basil, tomatoes, cucumbers, lettuce, beets, corn, and potatoes. Everything that you can purchase at Safeway or Albertson's today, Nanna grew in her yard—the cycle was endless; there was always something to pick!

Grandpa Franco was not to be outdone in the garden by his wife. No, he himself had favorite fruits and veggies, so he started planting fruit trees and some exotic trees that, although they did not produce fruit, served as a celebration of the flora that could and should be grown in California—somewhat of a snobbish celebration of nature's goodwill toward the Golden State, as California was then called. So up went fruit- and nut-producing trees. Toward the back of the acreage, you could find apricot, almond, walnut, peach, pear, and prune trees, and toward the front of the acreage, you would find such trees as eucalyptus, palm, and pepper (the latter creating umbrella-type branches that provided a great deal of much-needed shade in the summer). The latter three varieties are still located on the old family property. All the fruit trees however were cut down to make room for development.

Back to the family; Steve also found a wife who would settle for two kids. Her name was Victoria DiDenti, and she was gorgeous. I don't know how Steve won her over, but somehow, he did. They lived in San Jose until the war started, and then they moved to San Francisco where most of the defense-related jobs were located. Steve and Victoria had two girls: my cousins Fay and Elaine. Fay is now retired and lives on the California coast with her husband, Manny. Manny is Spanish not Italian, causing that same family DG to talk more about ethnic origins. Some thought Fay inherited some natural attraction to Manny since he was Spanish—probably like her grandfather Franco. The discussions, as I mentioned before, never ended until death stepped in. Anyway, Fay and Manny now live somewhere near Santa Cruz, California. Elaine married a dentist, and they now live in Austin, Texas—more about Texas and the family diaspora later.

John, the Stanford graduate, married Frances Tragni's sister, Teresa. Again, families were tight then. When social activities are restricted primarily to ethnic gatherings, the inventory of opposite sex potentials is limited. This did not seem to discourage anyone. The boys and girls seemed happy with this arrangement, and I'm sure my uncles and aunts enjoyed life and tried to forget as often as possible the sexual advice their mother (my Nanna) tried to instill in them—again, refer to chapter 1 when reminded of sex.

Here's a photo of 5 of Nanna's kids. Back row, left to right: John, my Mother Mary, Steve, Katherine, and Sam. Josephine and Paul are missing. I believe this was taken after Paul's death, and Josephine was with her husband in San Francisco).

Prior to prohibition life was sweet for the Italians in the Santa Clara Valley. Every Family with sufficient property to do so produced their own wine. Everything changed when the Volstead Act was approved by congress in 1920. The act permitted families to continue to produce their own wine as long as it was not intoxicating wine. If produced as fruit juice, it would be legal, but if it were 12 percent by volume, or intoxicating, then you were violating the law. Italian Families did not understand that, nor could they even begin to comprehend the rationale behind such a ridiculous law, so they continued smiling at inspectors and continued to stomp out the same old vintage they produced before the congressional act with the German-sounding name came into effect. Nanna was lamenting again that the Germans were going to start another war, and it would be miserable to conduct the war without wine.

My future Pedone grandfather, whose name I carry, thought it was a splendid act. He, and most of the Ranchers he contracted with, had vats full of wine and all the equipment and ingredients necessary to continue production, so with a slight blink of the eye and a handshake understood by all Sicilians, Grandpa Pedone went into the business of bootlegging. Their territory covered most of the San Francisco Bay area and even further south down to Salinas, Watsonville, Santa Cruz, and Monterey. I'm almost certain that if they had wanted to expand they could have easily done so, based on the continuing demand from those

European immigrants who downed a couple of glasses of fruit juice with every meal except breakfast, but Grandpa kept his cool and operated only where he was well known. I guess, in a way, this could have been a mistake. Regardless of what approach he used, he and his compatriots were breaking the law while making large sums of money, and money as we all know is the root of all evil. The money being made was also drawing attention to my future grandfather from other parts of the United States—that in itself was a big mistake.

In the meantime, Nanna and Franco did not totally approve of Mr. Pedone's fledging new business. They were concerned that my future grandfather Pietro was neglecting pruning opportunities in favor of wine production. They also sensed that what he was doing was illegal. Again, Nanna made reference to the Tedesci (Germans) who were obviously responsible for this silly act anyway, and why was America listening to this war-mongering German by the name of Volstead? Hadn't the Americans learned enough from World War I? Couldn't the Americans begin to see that Volstead was in league with this new emerging mad man in Germany by the name of Hitler? Couldn't the Americans see that Volstead and Hitler were working together to start World War II? "Che peccato," she would say (What a pity.). She also mentioned that these war mongers were influencing an Italian by the name of Benito Mussolini, and if he (Mussolini) did not change soon, he would be just like them; Nanna knew what she was talking about!

Nevertheless, despite Pietro Pedone's illegal activities, life for my Sicilian ancestors continued as normal as possible considering that a new threat to the United States by the name of Depression was on the horizon and beginning to show its ugly head. It all began with the crash of '29.

CHAPTER 9

PHYSICAL REMEDIES—BOWEL MOVEMENTS

Nanna's remedy of choice for ailments not associated with the skin was for one to have a hearty bowel movement. If assistance was required to achieve the necessary movement, then the consumption of mass quantities of Phillips Milk of Magnesia was strongly recommended—Nanna was a living commercial for Phillips. She took it herself every day; the blue bottle had its place of distinction on the kitchen counter near where the spoons and forks were kept—in other words, close at hand. I can see her now in my mind's eye downing two tablespoons of that white sickening stuff every day. Because of this, you won't find any Phillips in our house.

Nanna believed that food should exit the body as soon as possible. Time for digestion was secondary to the need to keep that stuff moving. I think Nanna herself suffered from irritable bowel syndrome because when not inspecting the house for cleanliness or harvesting fruit and veggies from the north 40, Nanna could be found on the throne, if you know what I mean. Oh, I guess that's not completely true; she did spend a great deal of time in the kitchen preparing delicious meals. But those meals were expected to leave the body as soon as possible. Thanks Nanna. Because of your early training, I now take Metamucil daily, and everything is turning out just fine, thank you!

As I mentioned before, Nanna's medical specialty was skin ailments. She could cure boils, rashes, carbuncles, and things of that nature overnight, primarily with salves made of nopal (no-*pahl*). But when it came to any other ailment her recommendation was to take a hearty bowel movement. Perhaps this is why most of her Italian women friends would seldom ask Nanna for medical advice beyond skin treatment. More of Nanna's remedies will be mentioned later.

CHAPTER 10

THE DEPRESSION

The Depression was not that difficult for Italian families in San Jose, California. They came to America with a sense of self-reliance and self-preservation. They knew how to grow and gather and accumulate their own food stuff. Give an Italian/Sicilian flour, and they will give you back bread, pasta, and cookies. Give them earth, and they will supply you with every vegetable known to man and then some. Italians, especially Sicilians, did not purchase canned foods from grocery shelves—what they couldn't can in Mason Jars or hang to preserve in the basement was not part of their daily meals. Their suffering during the depression was primarily due to the fact that they could not attend the movies as often as they would have liked.

The kids, led by Paul, would be out scrounging money—one way or the other. Collecting bottles for one or two cents exchange became a full-time job as they ranged—out beyond their neighborhoods, but not to the oriental neighborhoods.

They remembered their mother's advice very well, and none of them desired to wind up in a Chinese or Japanese soup, so they primarily concentrated on areas where white, Anglo-Saxon Mericans lived. They did very well in their scrounging. Wearing their well-worn, suspendered overalls, they conveyed the image of undernourished and deprived minorities and won the hearts and minds of the Merican communities. I overstretched the pronunciation here because "Mericans" was a term Nanna used. The kids spoke English very, very well, especially when asking for money or seeking some type of work for money.

The Depression favored ranchers over merchants. People in the east wanted the fruits and veggies grown in California—somewhat like the movie *East of Eden*, starring James Dean. Produce was prized in the east, so ranchers and those that supported ranching, such as my two grandfathers, did okay—their work was uninterrupted. Those people that did not work directly in the field, tending the trees or picking the fruit, wound up working in the canneries, canning fruit for transport to the east and other areas of the world. So with private gardens flourishing and orchard and cannery work readily available, the Portera and Pedone families did very well, especially in comparison to those less fortunate in the midwest or the east coast. Life continued to be good in Nanna's kitchen.

Meanwhile back at the orchards, where my future grandpa Pietro Pedone worked, much of the effort was now devoted to stomping on grapes and producing fruit juice with an alcoholic content of 12 percent or more. Demand for this unlabeled and genetically unmodified juice was skyrocketing. Local ranchers began harvesting as many grapes as they did apricots and prunes. They worked feverishly to help supply Mr. Pedone with the ingredients he and his colleagues need to produce the bottled stuff that was bringing in more money than fruits and veggies could provide. So this illegal business in agricultural biotechnology prospered and grew. My future grandfather was unknowingly also working hard to become a target for law enforcement as well as for Mafia-connected mobsters who were taking notice from a far-off city by the name of Chicago.

Business grew for Grandpa Pedone. The Italian word for "grandfather" varies from the Italian name for "grandmother" by one letter—one is masculine and the other feminine. Drop the *a* in "nonna" and add an *o* at the end and you have "nonno." Italian is truly "la lingua bella" (the beautiful language). So Nonno Pedone whom I never would meet became a very wealthy godfather amongst Sicilians in San Jose. He wore the ring well and invited all those who wished to kiss it as often as they would like, and apparently, they all liked it because he really did become the godfather of San Jose Sicilians. Like all godfathers, he would also become one very big target for not only the law but with other less fortunate godfathers.

Let's keep in mind that there was no social security in America during the Depression and during the Prohibition era. Families either found a way to make ends meet, or they suffered the consequences. Some of our Republican friends would like it that way today, but I personally believe that paying a tax during your working years to benefit your nonworking years is a stroke of genius.

The oncoming Depression and the threat of war in the air held little meaning for my cousins and me. Life was good in San Jose, and as long as we had each other to play with and as long as our families were happy, we were happy. Our families would gather at Nanna's on Sundays, and while we cousins were playing outside, the women would be in the kitchen cooking with Nanna—well, that is, they would be cooking, and Nanna would be giving the orders. "No," she would say to this ingredient or that and "Stir this while it boils," or "Stop, you are overcooking that!" Nanna's orders didn't seem to bother my aunts. When Nanna would scream an order, they would nod their heads, look at each other, with smiles on their faces, and continue what they were doing before Nanna yelled at them. Nanna, however, kept a straight face and continued to bark instructions. It was a routine we all loved to watch and hear.

When the tables were set (there was always more than one table), the women would yell for everyone to come sit down, and the feast would begin. We cousins would eat delicious foods until we could hardly move, and when we did move, it was to catch the electric street car that would take us to the movies in downtown San Jose. The street car stopped right in front of Nanna's house on San Carlos Street. The fare to ride the street car was next to nothing—it cost about ten cents per kid round trip, and we didn't use money; we used tokens. I don't recall exactly the cost because our parents gave us tokens that they purchased at a discount—the more tokens you purchased, the cheaper the amount, so travel to and from downtown San Jose was very affordable.

When the automobile industry started developing in Detroit, the market target was apparently California, so all the street car tracks were torn up, and roads widened to accommodate the automobile, which was very popular with Californians who could afford one. The street car tracks were torn up and sold to Japan, and the big joke after Pearl Harbor was that Japan was returning the steel street car tracks to us in the form of bombs dropped on our ships anchored at Pearl—probably a lot of truth to that. Travel by street car was very affordable, and they used little energy in comparison to the automobile, but the American mind-set locked onto the auto, and the rest is history. There are now thirty-six million people living in California, and most of the families have two or more cars, so you do the math. Whenever I think of the demand for gasoline in California, I think of the affordability of the street car and how little energy they used in comparison to the automobile.

Attending the movies with my cousins was a joy. I usually wound up going with the girls instead of the guys who didn't want their little cousin Peter tagging along—the girls, however, didn't mind, and I think they rather liked the idea of chaperoning a little male cousin. The problem with that was they never wanted to watch cowboy movies with Roy Rogers or Gene Autry. All they wanted to see were mushy movies like *Stormy Weather* starring Lena Horne. We would stop at the 5 and 10 Cents Store and purchase popcorn before we went into the movies. The ushers at the theatres didn't seem to mind it if you brought your own popcorn in. We saved a nickel by not purchasing the popcorn at the movies—it cost 15 cents there, and only 10 cents at Woolworths.

As I said before, San Jose at this time smelled of prunes and apricots. It was a typical central California town, ala American Graffiti. There were three major movie theatres in town: the Fox, which was considered the best and the most expensive; the Mission, which was second to the Fox, and the Padre, which held third place in terms of recent movie releases and cost for admission. When WWII broke out, my cousins and I were among the first to see the movie *Bataan*, starring Robert Taylor and Lloyd Nolan; it surprised us that the movie first appeared at the Padre, not the Fox. We were glued to our seats watching Robert Taylor mow down the charging Japanese with his Tommy gun, then later his machine gun. We liked the movie so much we went back to see it three times. At the end of the third performance, I think any one of us could have repeated all the lines of all the major characters. This was standard procedure for all the kids our age during the war in San Jose. We saw all the movies several times over, and we all helped raise money to fight the war by collecting newspapers, bacon grease, and scrap metal. We wore our play helmets as we did all this.

CHAPTER 11

NONNO PEDONE

"He's a wonderful man," said Nanna Portera on many occasions, "but when he's drunk, he's like a German!" I guess Nanna was right because my dad told me later in life that Nonno Pedone was both verbally and physically abusive to his wife Salvatrice (my other nanna) and all his children. He was especially abusive at the dinner table and allowed no one to speak unless he spoke to them first. Wow, I guess I'm fortunate to have been born two years after his murder. Everyone seemed to agree that when Nonno was sober, he had a heart of gold, but when drinking, he became a monster—a delightful dichotomy. I guess if you wanted to be around Nonno Pedone, you'd best do it in the morning before he started sipping in the afternoon with his cohorts in crime because after a few snorts, he was bulletproof, or so he thought. I guess those who murdered him reasoned that way because they did hit him in late afternoon.

Nonno was very big for a Sicilian. He stood six feet, two inches tall and weighed 290 pounds. Much of that was muscle; he did work hard and was not a stranger to strenuous, back-breaking work. The men he contracted with loved him because he would jump right in there and help them prune and trim trees and haul away branches and other ranching debris. But he did have a temper, and when it hit, you'd best be far away. As handsome and big as he was, he was bound to be a hit with the ladies, and it was well known that he did more than prune trees for the many ranching wives he encountered. At home, he fathered eight children, and God knows how many others throughout the San Francisco Bay area. During the late twenties, there were many big and scrapping, young Sicilian kids running around the Bay area that looked a great deal like Nonno, and it was reported that his funeral drew hundreds. You can see from the photo below how big Nonno was, especially in comparison to his male children. My father, Mario John Pedone, standing first in the back line on the left, was the tallest of the men children at five foot, ten inches, making him one of Nonno's favorite punching bags.

Pedone Family members. Back row, left to right: Mario John Pedone (my dad); Nanna Pedone, holding her youngest and final child, Peter. Next is Nonno Pedone (nice sober—mean drunk). Last in top row is Uncle Joe (Giuseppe) Pedone. First row, left to right: Caterina (married name, Kay Pezzolo); Aunt Mary (married name, Mary Conlin), Aunt Nancy (married name, Nancy Conlin), Aunt Julia (married name, Julia Arias), and finally, Uncle Sam, whose given name was Santo, but everyone called him Sam.

Nonno Pedone was well established in San Jose by the time the Porteras arrived. He was there at the train depot to greet the Porteras upon their arrival from Buffalo. He was more than among the crowd; he was the man in charge, setting an early image of himself for the Porteras as the leader (godfather) of the San Jose Italians. I think they knew that before they arrived from Buffalo, but Nonno Pedone wanted to ensure that there was no doubt. He was kind and generous to the Porteras and remained that way until the day he was murdered.

His murder happened late in the afternoon of December 28, 1932. He needed gas, so he drove his car to the Shell service station on the corner of San Carlos and Park Avenues in San Jose. My father, who had wanted to take a ride with his dad, was with Nonno when he was shot. The assassin, whom my father could not identify later, came out of nowhere and pulled a large caliber pistol out of his pocket and shot my grandfather several times in the head to ensure he would not survive. To finish the job and to ensure there were no witnesses, the assassin also shot my father once in the neck. He would have shot my father more times, but he either ran out of bullets or thought it best to get the hell out of there. Fortunately for my dad, the bullet missed his carotid vein by a hair, and although he must have appeared to be a bloody mess to the assassin, he survived after a month or so in the county hospital. Dad was never quite the same after that; he enjoyed being looked after, and his work history was punctuated with frequent spells in the hospital for one thing or the other—he became, more or less, a medical burden on the family.

The San Jose police force could not solve my grandfather's murder. The gas station attendant never saw the assassin, and there were no witnesses other than my father, who was too traumatized to remember much, so the case remains unsolved today, some eighty years later. I doubt seriously if the San Jose police department or the FBI were then, or are now, worried about it. To them, it was just another case of one minority group member killing another or, better yet, the Mafia hitting one of their own. We'll never know. The Pedone family has many theories as does the discussion group (DG) mentioned earlier. They now had something else to debate other than the nationality of Franco Portera. There is the thought that Nonno was murdered by a Chicago Mafia hit man, but usually when that happens, the murder is preceded by some type of warning to the family, and in this case, there was none, and there is no family memory of any visits from members of eastern families connected with the Chicago Mafia. A more logical explanation according to the DG is that Nonno Pedone was murdered by a jealous Italian husband whose wife slept with Pietro Pedone once too often. In any event, he met his end quickly, perhaps so quickly that he never knew why or who either. Good-bye, Nonno, sorry I never got to meet you!

Naturally, life changed quickly for the Pedone clan. As soon as my father was released from the hospital, he, as well as his older brother Joe, dropped out of school and went to work in the orchards. My dad was going on eighteen years of age then, and his formal education was over. Education for the Pedone children ended at the eighth grade level, which was the state requirement at the time. Money was needed to feed and clothe the family, so education beyond the required state level was out of the question. None of the Pedone children made it beyond the eighth grade.

Meanwhile, back on the Portera Cacti Farm, my mother had reached age sixteen and the gleam in her eye for my dad John was growing brighter. Although my dad's full Italian name was Mariano John Pedone, everyone called him John, including my mother to be. Her name was Mary Joan Portera, and everyone called her Mary. Mary and John took every advantage to stare at each other whenever the families got together, which was frequently. Franco had reservations about his daughter marrying Pietro's son John for fear that whomever murdered Pietro but flubbed the job on John would try to make up for it by ensuring his death next time around (a legitimate concern for sure). So now the DG had something else to talk about, and that was whether or not Mary should be seeing John and vice versa. Mom and Dad (I'll call them Mom and Dad even though they had not married yet) were well aware of this concern by not only the DG but also by all family members not in the DG, so the pressure was coming from both sides to keep John and Mary apart. Now that I look back on the family folklore about this separation, I'm almost certain everyone knew that by continuing to apply this pressure, John and Mary would elope, and oh, how romantic that would be.

Mom and Dad: Mary Joan and Mariano John sometime in the early 1980's, shortly before celebrating their 50th anniversary in 1983. Guess they proved the DG wrong.

Sure enough, my mother- and father-to-be did not disappoint. Uncle Joe (dad's older brother) lent him his car, and mom and dad eloped to Reno, Nevada, for a quickie marriage. As I said, both families knew this was coming, so when they did return from Reno, all was forgiven, and a church wedding was planned (that would make the union legal in God's eyes according to the Catholic church). So on the December 3, 1933, my mother and father became legally wed. I was born twelve months and five days later.

The hardships facing Nanna Pedone and the Pedone children after the shooting death of her husband and their father brought out the best in them. The tenacity of the Pedones is legend today. They all proved to be responsible and productive citizens of the United States. The oldest daughter, Nancy, worked her way into the real estate business and prospered, but not until she assured herself that her mother, Salvatrice, was well taken care of. Social security was finally approved in the early thirties, so Aunt Nancy applied for and received approval for SSI on behalf of her widowed mother. Social security assistance, thanks to President Roosevelt, was on the way. Aunt Nancy would do the same later for my other Nanna—supposedly, the primary subject of this book, but it's hard to stay on tract when you are a Sicilian.

CHAPTER 12

NANNA'S OTHER REMEDIES

Got a sore throat? Nanna could cure that in microseconds with either a bottle of iodine or mercurochrome! Yes, they worked, and that's why you can't find them on drugstore shelves today (I guess). Well, no—I've heard that both of these curing liquids are used in the manufacture of methamphetamine so are therefore illegal to sell. I can't vouch for the authenticity of this statement, but that's what I hear from our local pharmacists whenever I attempt to purchase some. Anyway, back then, Nanna carried an ample supply of each liquid to swab our throats in the event of soreness. Picture kids with red, swollen throats running around the house complaining of sore throats. When this happened, they became moving targets for Nanna. She would grab us and ask us to "Apri il tuo falena ampia" (Open your mouth wide), and then in a blink of the eye, she would swab our throats with either concoction, whatever she had on hand, and after a few seconds, voila, pain and irritation *gone*! No kidding, I sometimes use that treatment on myself today, and *yes*, I do have some iodine secreted away—please don't tell the Gestapo.

Mustard Plaster: Now this is a treatment we all enjoyed because it meant being nestled comfortably in bed, covers up to your chin, and everyone in the house praying that you would soon be better. Mustard plaster is a poultice of mustard seed powder spread inside a protective dressing and applied to the chest or abdomen to stimulate healing. This definition is right out of Wikipedia! Nanna came way before Wikipedia and/or Google, but she would be very proud to know that others were aware of her formula. She varied this formula somewhat, depending on her analysis of the severity of the ailment. She sometimes combined a bit of flour with the mustard seed, and sometimes she added an egg or two; both were part of her pharmacy, and whatever concoction she decided to use, it worked! I can still feel the soothing heat of the pad sitting right there on my chest. Thanks, Nanna!

Ear Aches: Nanna could cure ear aches in fifteen minutes using an ancient formula called suction. No, she did not use her mouth. Instead, she wrapped a waxed cloth tightly around a thin stick (about the diameter of a pencil) forming a hollow tube once the stick was removed. She then stuck one end of the tube in your ear—careful not to go too far in—just enough to form a seal in the ear canal; then she would light the upper end of the tube (yes, set it on fire), and the burning waxy tube would suck out the crud that caused the ear ache in the first place. This process also applied heat directly to the inflamed area, which would help speed up the healing. When I explained this treatment to friends, they were shocked and vowed never to try it. Before my mother's death, I had an ear ache, and unbeknownst to my wife, I traveled to my mom's house for the treatment. In no time flat, the ear ache was gone. That was many years ago, and I haven't had an ear ache since. Thanks again, Nanna!

Enemas: This was a favorite treatment of Nanna's especially if she were mad at you. First, she would encourage us to have a bowel movement. If that didn't work and for some reason the dreaded white stuff didn't work, then Nanna would resort to *an enema!* If an Enema was inevitable, and you knew it was coming; then, we kids learned to really be nice to Nanna beforehand and offer her kisses and caresses. It sometimes worked as well as the enema would.

Head Colds: Nanna would boil water in a huge pot to create steam. Then when the steam started billowing out like a volcano, she would put a huge bath towel over our heads and force us to stick our heads in the pot directly over the steam and breathe in deeply. The towel, of course, served to trap as much steam as possible; it was either breathe steam or die. "Not deep enough," she would say as we tried to escape the cauldron she created but to no avail. We remained there, taking deep breathes until we almost passed out. Voila, it worked! She stood there behind us with hands on her hips, and when we smiled at her and said we felt much better, she would reply, "Uscire di qui." Get out of here.

It's been a little over fifty years since Nanna's passing, and I know there were more remedies; there had to be more because she had a cure for everything, but this will have to do for now.

CHAPTER 13

WORLD WAR II

When WWII broke out, Nanna's sons did not run to the recruiting office to enlist. Nanna held them back—literally held them back. "No son of mine," she reasoned, "is going to be killed by some German. There," she said, "the Tedesci [German's] have done it again, just as I predicted! Let the British kill them, not my sons!" Nanna was still too pissed off at the Germans to fully comprehend that it was the Japanese, not the Germans, that bombed Pearl Harbor. She reasoned that the Japanese were too backward and too weak-willed to take on the United States. She also believed that with their squinty eyes, they could not possibly see well enough to bomb anything or shoot straight like the Tedesci (Germans) could. So as far as Nanna was concerned, we were at war with Germany again, but not Japan.

The draft board did not agree with Nanna, and both John and Sam were drafted. John, the Stanford graduate, was immediately sent to officer's training school, and Sam was sent to the infantry basic training school at Ft. Benning, Georgia. Nanna was a mess—she wailed and moaned almost all day, and she was beyond consolation by any family friend or member. There was only one person that could help Nanna, and that was Jesus Christ. Jesus lived two blocks west of Nanna's house in a church named St. Martin's. When her son's were drafted, Nanna visited with Jesus and made him a promise. She said, "Dio [God], I promise to walk barefooted to your house every day and light two candles, and I will stay with you at least one hour a day if you will promise to deliver my sons home safely to me after this war. Please, Dio, let me do this!"

Nanna kept her promise to God, and for three years, from that day in 1942 when she made that promise until that day in 1945 when Sam returned safely home, she walked to St. Martin's and lit two candles and prayed to God for the safe return of her boys. Apparently, God liked what he saw in Nanna because Sam lived through the Normandy invasion and returned home safely without a scratch. John returned home safely also but with another wife. I won't dwell on this too long; suffice it to say that because of his education and his Stanford credentials, John was placed in the intelligence corps and served behind the front lines where he lived a rather luxurious life interrogating Italian and German prisoners of war. There, in a small Italian village, he met and fell in love again with a beautiful Italian/Austrian woman named Joan—tough luck for Teresa who waited for him at home. I don't think Joan knew that John was married when they met, and after she became pregnant, it no longer mattered.

When the war ended, John came home to divorce Teresa, and of course, he broke Nanna's heart as well. He left Teresa and their two boys and rejoined his unit in Italy. He made a career of the army and retired with the rank of lieutenant colonel sometime in the 1960s. He and his new wife, Joan, had four kids, and as I write this story, I have absolutely no idea where they may be. The war changed the world as much as it changed John, who did the unspeakable thing for a good Sicilian husband—he divorced his wife for another woman. He was blackballed by all except Nanna, who loved him deeply despite his transgression. My mother once told me that Nanna had to play the role of a very angry and upset mother in front of others, especially Teresa's parents, the Tragnis. "I cannot hate my son for something only God has the power to control." This is what Nanna had said to my mother. I guess John realized before Nanna died that she had forgiven him. John now lies in some long row at Arlington National Cemetery. His headstone reads: John Portera, LTC, USA.

Sam came home to his wife, Rosalie, and they wasted no time in having two sons, back to back. Sam did his mother proud and worked and provided for his wife and family. All in all, Nanna's daily barefooted walk to St. Martin's and back after her visit with God and Jesus did the trick. The family survived and was intact. The only shameful blot was that created by John, but Nanna forgave him in her heart; no one else did.

On many occasions, when we lived with Nanna and Franco, I had to walk to church with Nanna, but I could walk faster than she because I had shoes on, and she did not. When we arrived at St. Martin's, Nanna made me sit there alongside her in a pew. She would pray a little, then get up and light more candles and kneel before the statue of Jesus, where she cried and wailed as she pleaded with God for the life of her sons. Other worshipers in the church didn't seem to mind. As a matter of fact, every time Nanna wailed, they would join right in. I guess they also had sons in the army. I didn't worry about her crying too much; I worried more about my aching knees and butt that grew so tired while Nanna conversed with God and Jesus. Every time I tried to relax a bit and sit down instead of kneeling, she would give me a dirty look, and I would immediately return to my knees. I guess that's why I don't go to church anymore.

Nanna's husband, Frank, the Spaniard, missed all this. He died in June of 1939, not long before the Germans started the war by bombing Poland. Frank worked steadily and provided well for his family until a month before his death when it became obvious that his will to live could not compete with the cancer in his lungs. He died in his bed at home, and Nanna and her family buried him where all San

Jose Italians are buried: Santa Clara Catholic Cemetery, the final resting place for most of my family, including my parents. There was no mention of his nationality on his tombstone, only his name and the date of his birth and death. The score was now cancer 6, loved ones 0.

World War II changed the family forever. Sons and daughters realized there was a world out there other than that one found in the Sicilian kitchen. The world was at their feet. There was money to be had; get an education and go to work. Save your money, use birth control, and enjoy life. Work eight hours a day, five days a week, take a vacation, and fly to…well, anywhere you wanted to, including Palermo, Sicily, if you felt like it. And one need not stay in San Jose for the rest of his or her life. There were forty-seven other states out there where one could perhaps find a better job than one offered in San Jose; perhaps the world and especially the United States could be greener on the other side. Yes indeed, the world had changed. No more stick shifting—you can have your dynaflow transmission and three-bedroom home for just a small down payment, and if you were a veteran like Sam, you could use your GI Bill. America is great. Thank you, God and Jesus! We are going to experience the American dream. The family diaspora was about to begin.

CHAPTER 14

LIFE IN SAN JOSE—PART 2

Nanna moved in with us sometime in 1946. I was twelve then, and by now, I had a sister and a brother. I enjoyed being the only child until 1942 when my sister was born; then after her birth, I realized how lucky I had been without either a sister or brother. My brother arrived in 1944 to round out the family at five. I now believe both were conceived as a surety that my dad would not be drafted. Either that or my mother coaxed dad into it. She felt rather guilty being a Sicilian with only one child. I, on the other hand, thought it spoke volumes for intelligent family management. Nanna's moving in with us upped the family count to six, meaning I had to share my bedroom with Nanna. No more playing with myself that's for sure.

Nanna was in her sixties now. She had been living alone since Sam's marriage, and the family thought it would be best to sell off the cactus farm and split the money among all the Portera offspring. What a huge mistake. I believe they sold the property for some $25,000 back then, and today, that property is worth a conservative five million! But with World War II now history and all the family safely back in San Jose (except John), the prevailing mind-set was to sell and split the loot and pass Nanna off to whomever felt like taking her on or—as still happens many times even today—whoever was naive enough to take on that responsibility without the family agreeing to some type of financial arrangement as to how much each would contribute for her upkeep. But my dad felt like a hero one day and offered to take Nanna in without the aforementioned determination of a fair financial split. No wonder everyone immediately agreed to my dad's generosity. So the cacti-ringed property was sold, and Nanna came to inspect our house on a long-term basis.

SOME HUMOROUS INCIDENTS

Nanna was afraid of heights and hills. There are many hills in San Francisco, and her daughter Josephine lived on one of them. We would drive to San Francisco at least once a month for a big cioppino feed with the Russo family—it was usually a one-day turn around trip, and the drive was enjoyable on the Bayshore Highway between San Jose and Frisco as we all called it then. Nanna would not stay in the car as Dad approached hills. She not only did not like hills, she did not like being at an angle sitting in the backseat as Dad and the car negotiated the hill. Nanna being so short could not see where the car was going. So she demanded to be let out of the car as Dad approached each hill; she would then walk up the hill, and Dad would pick her up there. This added at least an hour to each trip to San Francisco. I think of her every time I drive up a hill in the city by the bay.

Nanna liked Fisherman's Wharf where all the Italian Fishermen worked and sold their catches. She liked to flirt with all the older Italians and tease the younger ones. Her favorite trick on the wharf was negotiating the price of a crab. Anything over 75 cents meant negotiation. She would say such things as: "Do you realize how old and poor I am?" Until the fishermen got to know her better, they would say something like "No, signora, how much can you afford?" She often got a whole crab for 25 cents. Her trump card, if a merchant was not willing to meet her demand, was to offer 25 cents for a crab missing a leg or two; this made everyone happy, and we would walk off with crabs that were drawing disability pay.

Nanna loved kids. I think she liked other people's kids better than she liked her own kids, and that included all my friends and all the kids in our neighborhood. Nanna would bake bread, and the smell of that bread baking wafted through the neighborhood like a Kansas tornado, and the kids were drawn to our home like a magnet. She knew they would be coming, so she would have the olive oil and salt already for them. Back then, there was no neighborhood concern as to where your kids might be. The neighbors had no worries—not only was Nanna feeding them, Nanna was also babysitting them. The neighbors knew their kids were in good hands. This of course made me very popular in the area. Not only was I sought after for kick the can games, but also as a buddy close to his Nanna, who had all the bread. An added footnote so to speak: Nanna was all talked out by now—she had no worldly lesson to pass onto the neighbor kids as she did her grandchildren, such as I. None of my neighbors realized that virginity in women was a godly requirement nor did they ever learn that every war in the world was started by the Germans. They lucked out I guess; they got all they wanted to eat, and they didn't have to listen to a lesson one. All they received from Nanna was smiles and Italian mumblings: "Qui e il tuo pane. Sei cosi carina, ecc., ecc. Ora andare a giocare." Here's your bread. You are so cute, etc., etc. Now go play.

"What did she say to you?" the kids would later ask each other. "I don't know," was frequently the reply. But sometimes, one of the neighbor girls would say, "She thinks I'm cute. I like her!"

CHAPTER 15

NANNA'S FINAL DAYS

To judge something you must be there.
—Bronislaw Malinowski

As I look at the photos I have placed in this memoir and as I look back on my life with Nanna, I enter the world of mixed emotions. As a child, she was my pillar of strength. She provided me with the hugs, kisses, and affection a growing child needs; Nanna was always there. My parents, although they loved me very much, were preoccupied with finding work and coping with the downside of the Depression. By the time my parents settled into married life and achieved the working security they required, I was already a young boy who had been raised by his grandmother.

As a boy, I gave no consideration to what Nanna had endured and accomplished in her life. She had no formal education, but despite that, she was very knowledgeable about everything that was important to know in those days, to assure the survival of her beloved family, including: how to assure that a lone woman travelling with three small children obtains adequate shelter and plentiful food on a 1913 tramp steamer; how to grow, cook, and preserve sufficient amounts of nutritious food for a family of nine; how to properly grow, prepare, or purchase and use the correct herbs, plants, and/or packaged medicines necessary to treat illness and disease; that cleanliness and sanitation were the *only* ways to prevent disease; how to persuade God not to let her sons die in the war; how to keep the horny Italian adolescent males in her family from knocking up the horny, young Italian girls in the family and in the rest of her Italian neighborhood; and, perhaps most importantly, how to make the children in her family feel warm and happy and loved. I now realize she did all that!

On the other hand, many of the things Nanna taught me and my cousins were based on teachings she had received from her illiterate parents, or learned from the teachings of Catholicism in the rural Sicilian countryside.

Catholicism taught her the simple things of life: you are born, you are baptized and you marry young as a virgin; you may have as many children as God wants, and you die. What's complicated about that? Although Nanna had the best interests of her loved ones in mind, much of her teaching was based on values and morals founded in nineteenth century Sicily. Although my cousins and I eventually learned that many of Nanna's teachings were wrong; it was very difficult to overcome the ideas, values, and morals that are planted in the minds of young people. Continued racial prejudice throughout the world is a good example of beliefs that are planted forever in the minds of the young. Will the peoples of the world ever overcome this hateful tendency?

Remember Nanna's promise to Jesus and God? In exchange for returning her son's safely home from WWII, Nanna promised to walk barefooted to church every day and to spend at least one hour per day in conversation with Jesus and God. It worked for her—Sam came home safely, and John chose to remain in the army after divorcing his wife for an Italian woman he discovered during the war. *So be it*, she thought, *God has his ways, and if God wanted John to meet and marry another woman, that was that!* All was eventually forgotten, except the price Nanna had to pay for the help she received from God and Jesus.

As a result of her daily barefooted walk to church for those three or so years, a black, cancerous sore began to appear on the bottom of her right foot. She never mentioned it to anyone because it was on her body, and her body belonged to only God, her, and her husband. No one else, not even the best of doctors were going to see any part of Nanna's body—that is, until she lay there dying, then she didn't care.

The amputation of Nanna's right foot did not save her from the deadly melanoma cancer that invaded her body from the foot up. She died heavily medicated in June 1965 at the age of eighty-two or so while Sandy and I were stationed in West Germany. The last time we saw Nanna was June 1962. We miss her very much, and I come close to shedding tears every time I walk by a bakery where the smell of freshly baked bread hits me. I immediately envision a piece of warm bread with olive oil and a bit of salt on it. Thanks for the wonderful memory, Nanna, and buona notte.

CHAPTER 16

FAMILY DIASPORA—THE END OF THE OLD WAYS

The past is nothing more than a bucket of ashes.

—Carl Sandberg

Growing up with my cousins was a blessing I never realized until I became an adult and finally understood what life was all about. My cousins and I had everything—we had family togetherness, family gatherings, and a love for each other that I really don't see in family structures today. My cousins are mostly gone now, and those that remain are as totally absorbed in their own little world as I am wrapped up in mine. Those of us still alive live hundreds of miles from one another. I have cousins in North Carolina, Virginia, Pennsylvania, Florida, Texas, Ohio, Washington, and California. I have second and third cousins I will never meet or get to know. As I talk with my friends today, I realize my family is no different from other American families. We have spread ourselves all over the map.

The first generation Americans, that is my Portera and Pedone aunts and uncles are almost all gone; the Porteras are indeed gone, but I still have one aunt and one uncle still kicking around from the Pedone clan. All my aunts and uncles did well. They survived the war; they worked hard and prospered, and their children are responsible adults living life just as all Americans do—too many fast-food stops and not enough Nannas to make hot Italian/French bread to eat, and yes, they all walk around texting!

My father and mother struggled through life. They both worked until retirement age, which was about the same time that I graduated from high school and faced the decision as to whether or not to attend college. I was finally given some encouragement from mom and dad to attend college because they didn't want me to be a working fool as they put it for the rest of my life. "Don't be a working jackass like me," Dad said.

"Get an education—keep your hands clean, not dirty and calloused like mine!" Mom nodded her head up and down in agreement, so off to college I went, where I met the love of my life and future wife, Sandra Louise Leak. Sandy (as we called her) and I have now been married fifty-one years and have two grown children, five grandkids, and one great-grandson. We are proud of our lives and our accomplishments.

Sandy and I wanted something different in life. We wanted to see the world. California was closing in on us; people were moving to the Golden State in huge numbers and at a rapid pace, the fruit trees were being replaced by suburbia, and the streets and roads were becoming parkways and freeways. We both wanted to move away from the destruction of our state and perhaps visit Europe and perhaps see other parts of the United States we had only read about. So I entered reserve officers training, was commissioned in the army, and, like my Uncle John, I was off to Europe. But instead of looking for a wife there, I thought it best to take with me the one I already had. Our decision to see the world and make a career of the army was a good one, even though I spent one year in Vietnam. I completed my career in the early eighties, pooped around with several nondescript civilian jobs, and fully retired in 1996. Sandy earned her master's degree in family counseling, worked for a couple of counties in the Northwest, and retired in 2002.

In addition to wanting to see the world, I had a driving need to leave San Jose—I wanted to break the mold; I did not want to be another San Jose Italian growing up to work on some ranch or farm or to be a produce clerk in some super market like so many of my Italian relatives and friends. Oh, these were honorable occupations but not for me. I wanted a college education, and after graduation, I wanted to do something non-Italian. And so it worked out, and now instead of seeking new travel adventures, my wife and I look for restaurants recommended by Guy Fieri.

I know this is a quick read covering over one hundred years of life in two Sicilian/Italian immigrant families. Although we are a nation of immigrants, being an immigrant in our country has never been easy. Yes, my maternal and paternal families had their difficulties, but nothing as difficult as many of the immigrants back then and even today. In my opinion, there is as much prejudice today as there was back in the early 1900s. Today, as then, immigrants receive the brunt of the blame for unemployment and violence, and they are characterized as disrespectful of the institutions most valued by white, Anglo Saxon Americans. It's not fair, but until families start teaching their children to be respectful of all races, nationalities, and religions, nothing will change. We were once proud to be the melting pot. Today, however, we seem to have thrown the pot out.

Talk of Grandpa Frank Portera's nationality or point of origin ended long ago. Today, if I were to mention nationality to any family member, all I would receive in return would be a blank stare. Who cares anymore? Nanna and Franco are fading memories to all but a few now. The prevailing thought today, among our young ones, is who has the latest iPod, computer, or Smart phone. No one calls anymore just to chat or to ask what we are eating this evening. No one calls to suggest a family gathering on the coast. We really don't know each other anymore. As I write this, I think about all the warm bread we ate when we gathered as a family, and I realize there's no one to call anymore to see if they want to break bread together. Oh well, that's life; instead of calling someone, I'll just get on the computer and check my e-mail. You know, I can't say I liked it better back then, but I can say the memories, ah yes, the memories, they are so damned beautiful.

ABOUT THE AUTHOR

Mr. Pedone was born and raised in San Jose, California, when, as he puts it, *it smelled of prunes and apricots.* Today, San Jose is the tenth largest city in the United States and the center of the nation's computer industry. The smell of prunes and apricots is long gone. The Santa Clara Valley, as it was once called, is better known today as the Silicon Valley.

During his college years, Mr. Pedone enlisted in the Army Reserve Officers Training Program (ROTC) and, upon completion, was commissioned a second lieutenant of infantry in 1962. He completed a twenty-six-year career in the army and retired with the rank of lieutenant colonel. He served as a combat company commander and staff officer in Vietnam during the period April 1966 to April 1967. During his tour of duty in Vietnam, he was awarded the combat infantryman's badge, bronze star, and air medal. The air medal is awarded to infantrymen after completing thirty-two assaults on landing zones controlled by the enemy.

Captain Pedone during a 1966 combat operation in the jungles of Vietnam.

While in the service, Colonel Pedone advanced his education and received a masters degree in business and labor relations from Golden Gate University in San Francisco, California. When he was promoted to the rank of major, the army assigned him to the Command and General Staff College located at Fort Leavenworth, Kansas. Upon successful completion of this course, Major Pedone was awarded a certificate of completion, and shortly thereafter, he was promoted to the rank of lieutenant colonel.

Today, Mr. Pedone enjoys the Western sport of Cowboy Action Shooting where participants shoot old-time firearms used during the western migration in the United States after the Civil War (1865–1899). Participants in Cowboy Action Shooting dress in authentic clothing of that era, and they select a character name that goes along with the persona they wish to emulate while playing the game. Because of his interest in writing and storytelling, Mr. Pedone selected the *handle* of Palaver Pete—Palaver meaning one who loves to write, as well as *casting about tall tales of the early west.* Mr. Pedone is a contributing writer to the *Cowboy Chronicle*, a monthly newspaper distributed by the mother organization of Cowboy Action Shooting, the Single Action Shooting Society located in Edgewood, New Mexico.

Mr. Pedone as seen in his Cowboy role of Palaver Pete.

Mr. Pedone lives in Sunriver, Oregon, with his wife of fifty-one years, Sandra Louise. He and Sandra have two adult offsprings, five grandchildren, and one great-grandson. Mr. Pedone will soon be introducing his second nonfiction book titled *Be Prepared to Stop*, a story about his travels around the United States and the interesting locations he and his wife have visited.